THE INTERVIEWER'S POCKETBOOK

By John Townsend

Drawings by Phil Hailstone

"An excellent, concise and well-organised guide to the art of interviewing."
H-J Jensen, Director, Personnel Flight Crews, SAS (Scandinavian Airlines System) Stockholm.

"The first **real** interviewing guide for managers I've come across."
F. Zumstein, Human Resources Manager, COSA Division, Caterpillar Overseas SA, Geneva.

"Very comprehensive and packed with confidence-building techniques which even the most experienced manager will find useful."
Rosalind Allison-Calvert, Director of Human Resources, ACNielsen Co. Ltd.

CONTENTS

PART 1: INTERVIEWING SKILLS
QUESTIONING TECHNIQUES

WORD OF WARNING

The great majority of interviewers ask very bad questions. Asking good questions is not a natural human talent. Our natural tendency in any kind of interview is to talk too much, to lead the interviewee towards our own way of thinking and to overload him or her with multiple questions.

The result is a very bad interview where the limited amount of information obtained is of poor quality.

Then we wonder why decisions taken on the basis of the information obtained turn out to be wrong!

QUESTIONING OR INTERACTIVE LISTENING?

In any interview situation there is a difference between questioning and interactive listening.

Questioning In a questioning situation the interviewer takes the initiative in deciding which kind of information he or she needs. The **way** in which the interviewer proceeds to ask for information may vary from empathetic questioning through interrogation to inquisition!

Interactive listening In the interactive listening mode the interviewer asks questions concerning **only** the information being provided by the interviewee (see page 24).

CLOSED & OPEN QUESTIONS

Closed   A closed question is one to which there is only one answer:
- 'What year was the Battle of Hastings?'
- 'Do you like spaghetti bolognese?'
- 'What kind of mainframe computer does your company use?'

Open   An open question is one to which there are many possible answers:
- 'What is your opinion on the current crisis?'
- 'How do you feel about working with flexitime?'
- 'What would you do if you won £1,000,000?'

QUESTIONING TECHNIQUES

MULTIPLE QUESTIONS

A multiple question is a string of several questions.

EXAMPLE

'Well, I have with me the captain of the French rugby team. Now tell me, what do you think of your chances in the next world cup now that New Zealand have lost their star goal kicker? Do you think it will set them back? And do you believe your present string of successes will continue? Also, how about England losing against Romania? Is this going to affect next year's tournament?'

WHEN TO ASK

Never! Why? Because when you ask a multiple question, the interviewee will only answer the last question or the easiest one! So, why not ask the last one or the easiest one?

QUESTIONING TECHNIQUES

LEADING QUESTIONS

These are questions that indicate the desired response.

EXAMPLE

'Oh, I see you started your career with XYZ International?'
'Yes.'
'Ah, good, and you were promoted after three years to district sales manager?'
'That's right.'
'Good - er - must have done a good job then?'
'Well, you know ...'
'Yes, oh, and then two years as regional manager?'
'Yes.'

WHEN TO ASK

Never! Why? Because the only way an interviewee can provide any high quality
information is by interrupting you or disagreeing with you.

PROBING QUESTIONS

These are closed questions seeking specific information you need.

EXAMPLES

- 'How old were you then?'
- 'What are the sales of ABC Ltd?'
- 'How many employees do you have working for you?'

WHEN TO ASK

- When you wish to probe for facts or details
- When the interviewee is rambling or talking too much

QUESTIONING TECHNIQUES

BLOCKBUSTING QUESTIONS

Blockbusting questions are closed questions which ask for more 'precision' in the information provided by the interviewee.

EXAMPLES

- Noun blockbuster - 'Which (noun) specifically?'

- Verb blockbuster - 'How (verb) exactly?'

- Universal block- - 'All? Never? Everyone?'
  buster

- Comparator - 'Compared to what?'

WHEN TO ASK

- When you need precise details on facts or actions

- As above

- After vague general statements such as 'all', 'never', 'none', 'everyone', 'always', 'nobody', etc

- After statements using vague comparisons such as 'better', 'increase', 'improve', 'less', 'more', 'efficient', etc

Based on McMaster and Grinder's Precision Model

QUESTIONING TECHNIQUES

'ABOUT' QUESTIONS

'About' questions are open questions that allow the interviewee to choose which information to provide.

EXAMPLES

- 'Tell me more about ...?'

- 'What do you think about ...?'

- 'How do you feel about ...?'

WHEN TO ASK

- At the beginning of an interview to get the interviewee talking

- When you wish to hear the interviewee's opinions, attitudes or beliefs

- As above

When in doubt ... ask 'about'

QUESTIONING TECHNIQUES

REFLECTIVE QUESTIONS

(ACTIVE LISTENING)

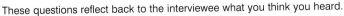

These questions reflect back to the interviewee what you think you heard.

EXAMPLES

- 'You seem to feel upset with ...?'

- 'If I understand you correctly you ...?'

- 'In other words, you don't ...?'

- 'You thought, perhaps, he was over-reacting?'

WHEN TO ASK

- With children!

- When an interviewee is emotionally involved with what is being discussed

- When the interviewee is being incoherent

- When you do not wish to influence the interviewee with your own opinions or beliefs

QUESTIONING TECHNIQUES

HYPOTHETICAL QUESTIONS

These are open questions that ask for information in a hypothetical situation.

EXAMPLES

- 'What would you do if ...?'

- 'Could we role-play this situation? I'll be the customer/student ...'

- 'What could have happened if ...?'

WHEN TO ASK

- When you wish to test creativity

- To test selling or public speaking skills

- When you wish to see how quickly/logically the interviewee thinks

QUESTIONING TECHNIQUES

CHALLENGE QUESTIONS

This type of open question challenges the interviewee to provide back-up information.

EXAMPLES

The Evidence Challenge:
- 'What will you accept as evidence of success?'

The Missing Link Challenge:
- 'What information are we still missing before we can ...?'

The Devil's Advocate Challenge:
- 'What would argue **against** what you're proposing?'

WHEN TO ASK

- To test interviewee's approach to objectives and targets

- To probe the interviewee's analytical and planning abilities

- A way of challenging an interviewee's objectivity

QUESTIONING TECHNIQUES

FRAMING QUESTIONS

This type of open question asks for information that fits into the framework of your discussion.

EXAMPLES

The Outcome Frame:
- 'What is the real outcome you're aiming at?'

The Backtrack Frame:
- 'How did you see things at the time?'

The Relevance Frame:
- 'Help me to see how this fits in with ...'

WHEN TO ASK

- To test planning ability and to probe reasons for actions

- To help put information 'in context'

- When you can't see why a point was brought up but want to get the interview back on track by giving the benefit of the doubt

QUESTIONING TECHNIQUES

SILENCE

Silence can be a useful questioning technique.

EXAMPLES	**WHEN TO USE**
• Up to 5 seconds' silence	• To allow interviewee to collect thoughts; courtesy
• 5-20 seconds' silence	• To encourage interviewees to share information they probably want to keep to themselves
• 20 seconds' silence or more	• To pressurise for confidential information or to obtain concessions/confessions

PART 1: INTERVIEWING SKILLS
<u>LISTENING</u>

LISTENING

LISTENING TEST

Quiz 1
A. Circle the term that best describes you as a listener:

- Superior
- Above average
- Below average
- Terrible
- Excellent
- Average
- Poor

B. On a scale of 0 -100 (100 = high) how would you rate yourself as a listener? ☐

Quiz 2
How do you think the following people would rate you (0 - 100) as a listener?

- Your best friend ☐
- A subordinate ☐

- Your boss ☐
- Your spouse ☐

- A business colleague ☐

16

LISTENING TEST ANALYSIS

QUIZ 1

A. 85% of all listeners questioned rated themselves as *average* or less. Fewer than 5% rate themselves as *superior* or *excellent*.

B. On the 0 - 100 scale, the extreme range is 10 - 90, the general range is 35 - 85, and the average rating is 55.

QUIZ 2

When comparing the listening self-ratings and projected ratings of others, most respondents believe that their *best friend* would rate them highest as a listener. And that rating would be higher than the one they gave themselves in Quiz 1 ... where the average was a 55.

How come? We can only guess that the best friend status is such an intimate, special kind of relationship that you can't imagine it ever happening unless you were a good listener. If you weren't, you and he or she wouldn't be best friends to begin with.

Going down the list, people who take this test usually think their *bosses* would rate them higher than they rated themselves. Now, part of that is probably wishful thinking and part of it is true. (We do tend to listen to our bosses better ... whether it's out of respect or fear or whatever doesn't matter.)

The grades for *colleague* and *subordinate* work out to be just about the same as the listener rated himself ... that 55 figure again.

But when you get to *spouse* ... husband or wife ... something really dramatic happens. The score here is significantly lower than the 55 average that previous profile-takers gave themselves. And what's interesting is that the figure goes steadily downhill. While newlyweds tend to rate their spouse at the same high level as their best friend, as the marriage goes on ... and on ... the rating falls. So, in a household where the couple has been married 50 years, there could be a lot of talk, but maybe nobody is really listening.

PRIMARY COMMUNICATIONS ACTIVITY

- We spend 80% of our waking hours in communications activities
- 45% of this time is spent listening
- Interviewees spend 60-70% listening
- Interviewers spend ?% listening!

PREPARING TO LISTEN

- As a professional interviewer you should always prepare yourself to listen by asking: 'What new things can I learn from this person?' Be selfish!

"There is no such thing as an uninteresting subject. There are only uninterested people." G.K. Chesterton

- Consider the 'listening barriers' (pages 20-22) and pinpoint your own bad habits.

- Avoid distractions. Find a quiet office and/or arrange to prevent telephone interruptions.

- Lean forward, establish sensitive eye contact (see page 36) and show you're ready to listen.

LISTENING BARRIERS

Here are nine behaviours that prevent us from becoming better listeners:

1. Scoring 'points' (Relating everything you hear to your own experience)
- Saying, 'Oh, that's nothing, you should have seen what happened to me last week!'
- Thinking, 'Mm! My kids are so much more intelligent than that!'

2. Mind reading (Predicting what the interviewee is really thinking)
- Saying to yourself, 'I bet that's not the real reason he left XYZ!'

3. Rehearsing (Practising your next lines in your head)
- Preparing your next 'clever' question and missing the present answer.

MORE LISTENING BARRIERS

4. Cherry picking   (Listening for a key piece of information - then switching off)
- Checking that an interviewee has IT experience and then not listening to the details.
- Ensuring that the interviewee's health seems OK but not listening to the proof.

5. Daydreaming
- You can think 4-6 times faster than people can talk. The temptation is to use the 'spare' time to daydream.

6. Labelling   (Putting an interviewee into a category before hearing all the evidence)
- Quickly dubbing an interviewee as a 'typical' accountant/salesman, etc.
- Not listening to an interviewee whom you've decided is a rambler, etc.

MORE LISTENING BARRIERS

7. Counselling   (Being unable to resist interrupting and giving advice)
- Saying, 'Why don't you try ...' or 'In my experience, the best ...'

8. Duelling   (Countering an interviewee's verbal advances with parries and thrusts of your own)
- Saying, 'Well, at least this department is never over budget!'
- Saying, 'You won't find people in this company acting like that!'

9. Side-stepping sentiment   (Countering expressions of emotion with jokes or hollow clichés)
- Saying, 'Well, it's not the end of the world, is it?'
- Saying, 'Stiff upper lip. Tomorrow's another day!'

NON-INTERVENTIONAL LISTENING

Non-interventional listening has its roots in Freudian psycho-analysis, in which the patient on the couch will gradually 'spill the beans' if only the analyst can keep quiet long enough! It is certainly a valid technique when faced with an interviewee who is emotionally disturbed or excited and who needs to let off emotional steam. In these cases, any kind of intervention on your part may be interpreted as an attack or criticism, or simply as an unwanted interruption, and thus distort the flow of information in some way.

However, in 'normal' situations, an interviewee who becomes aware of your non-committal silent technique may become wary to the extent of clamming up or, worse, distort the information in order to make it more palatable to their 'confessor'.

INTERACTIVE LISTENING

Here is a flowchart I've developed for all those who want to become better listeners. Details of each step can be found elsewhere in this Pocketbook.

Remember, when you're in the 'interactive listening' mode you let the interviewee provide the **areas** of information. You don't change the subject.

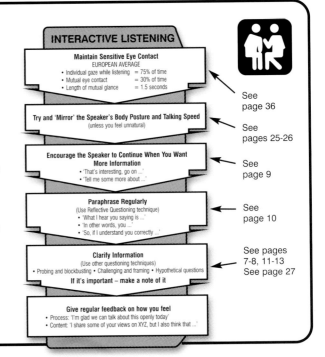

INTERACTIVE LISTENING

Maintain Sensitive Eye Contact
EUROPEAN AVERAGE
- Individual gaze while listening = 75% of time
- Mutual eye contact = 30% of time
- Length of mutual glance = 1.5 seconds

See page 36

Try and 'Mirror' the Speaker's Body Posture and Talking Speed
(unless you feel unnatural)

See pages 25-26

Encourage the Speaker to Continue When You Want More Information
- 'That's interesting, go on ...'
- 'Tell me some more about ...'

See page 9

Paraphrase Regularly
(Use Reflective Questioning technique)
- 'What I hear you saying is ...'
- 'In other words, you ...'
- 'So, if I understand you correctly ...'

See page 10

Clarify Information
(Use other questioning techniques)
- Probing and blockbusting • Challenging and framing • Hypothetical questions

If it's important – make a note of it

See pages 7-8, 11-13
See page 27

Give regular feedback on how you feel
- Process: 'I'm glad we can talk about this openly today'
- Content: 'I share some of your views on XYZ, but I also think that ...'

MIRRORING BODY POSTURE

When you are with someone you like you unconsciously adapt your body posture to theirs. You'll lean forward on the desk when they do, cross your legs as they do or put your elbow on the bar as they do.

Good listeners intuitively 'mirror' a speaker's body posture, whether they are best friends or not, because they know it helps rapport.

As you start practising to become a better interviewer, why not do it consciously? It soon becomes second nature!

ECHOING TALKING SPEED

Good interviewers pace the speed of their speech to that of the interviewee. Someone who is excited about something will speak rapidly and animatedly.

If you respond with a similar 'excited speed', the interviewee is more likely to continue giving useful information. If she or he is being cautiously slow/hesitant in speech delivery, then an 'echo' of that caution in your questions and comments will show your respect, courtesy and understanding of that person's feelings.

NOTE-TAKING

Should you take notes during an interview?

Generally speaking, yes - as long as you announce your intention to do so up front and as long as you are able to maintain sensitive eye contact.

You will obviously take more notes in a fact-finding interview than in a counselling interview.

Note-taking is proof to the interviewees that you are taking their information-giving seriously - but don't overdo it or it will make them feel as if they are at the police station: 'Anything you say will be taken down ...!'.

NOTES

PART 1: INTERVIEWING SKILLS
INTERPRETING BODY LANGUAGE

INTERPRETING BODY LANGUAGE

YOU CAN'T **NOT** COMMUNICATE

Research has shown that when someone gives a spoken message the listener's understanding and judgement of that message comes from:

7% WORDS

- Words are only labels and listeners put their own interpretation on speakers' words

38% PARALINGUISTICS

- The **way** in which something is said (ie: accent, tone, inflection, etc) is very important to a listener's understanding

55% FACIAL EXPRESSIONS

- What a speaker looks like while delivering a message affects the listener's understanding most

Research source - Albert Mehrabian

INTERPRETING BODY LANGUAGE

PARALINGUISTICS

If you are an average interviewer, 38% of your final evaluation of any interviewee will have been affected by the **way** that person spoke during the interview. Here are seven types of paralinguistics to listen for:

TYPE	INTERPRETATION
Timing	Short utterances may indicate shyness but may also depend on questions asked (ie: closed = short, open = long).
Tone/inflection	Convey emotions being felt by the interviewee and also help you identify the image she or he wishes to project.
Speech errors	All are indicators of anxiety or stress except 'ers' and 'ums' which simply indicate the interviewee is buying time.
Accent	Tells you where the interviewee comes from! Beware of your own prejudices!
Choice of words	Gives colour to speech and indicates level of education, attitude towards subject matter and degree of formality perceived.
Verbal 'tics'	Verbal mannerisms could indicate poor vocabulary, laziness, fashion influence, messy thinking or just plain habit.
Emphasis	Tonic accents on syllables and words signpost the real meaning (eg: 'I know how **you** feel about the situation').

TYPES OF BODY LANGUAGE

POSTURES & GESTURES

- How does interviewee use hand gestures? Sitting position? Stance?

EYE CONTACT

- How often do your eyes meet? For how long?

ORIENTATION

- How does interviewee position himself/herself to you?

PROXIMITY

- How close do you sit/stand to interviewee?

LOOKS/APPEARANCE

- Are looks/appearance important?

EXPRESSIONS OF EMOTION

- Can you trust facial expressions as signposts to emotion?

POSTURES & GESTURES: HANDS

STEEPLING

- Self-confidence (intellectual arrogance?)

HAND CLASP

- Anxious, controlled

NOSE TOUCH

- Doubt

'L' CHIN REST

- Critical evaluation

MOUTH BLOCK

- Resisting speech

33

POSTURES & GESTURES: SITTING

ARMS UP

- Reserved, defensive

ARM/LEG CROSS

- Closed, unconvinced

LEAN FORWARD

- Ready!

LEAN BACK

- Confident superiority

LINT-PICKING

- Disapproval

34

POSTURES & GESTURES: STANDING

THUMBS OUT

- In charge! Dominant

FIG LEAF

- Self-control, tense

ARMS OUT PALMS UP

- Open, sincere, conciliatory

TABLE LEAN

- Authoritative, involved

LEAN ON

- Unthreatened, casual belongingness

EYE CONTACT

Recent studies by Michael Argyle show that during the average European conversation:

- The listener looks at the speaker for 75% of the time
- The speaker looks at the listener for 40% of the time
- Both look each other in the eye for 30% of the time
- The length of each mutual glance is only 1.5 seconds

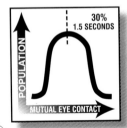

So, if the middle of the curve represents how most people establish and maintain eye contact during an interview, both you and the interviewee will 'feel' that any more or any less eye contact is abnormal. Is it good or bad? Only you and they can judge according to your personalities.

Tip Stick to the norm!

INTERPRETING BODY LANGUAGE

ORIENTATION

In most interview situations (except fact-finding) you should try and avoid sitting behind your desk and move to a less formal setting around a coffee or conference table.

In this diagram, if you sit in position X and if the interviewee can choose which position to take, that choice will indicate how he or she perceives the nature of the interview and, perhaps, how friendly or intimidating **you** seem.

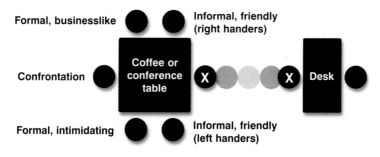

PROXIMITY

The average European feels comfortable in an interview when the distance between the two parties is 46 centimetres!

However, this average hides four separate components which people intuitively use in calculating their 'comfort zone':

1. Upbringing   People brought up in rural areas need more space.

2. Nationality/culture   Mediterranean people prefer closer contact - and a lot of touching!

3. Perceived mutual status   People keep further away from those they believe have a higher status than themselves.

4. Sex   Women talking to other women stay 15 cm closer than when talking to men.

When in doubt, stick to 46 cm!

INTERPRETING BODY LANGUAGE

LOOKS/APPEARANCE

Research indicates that clothes do indeed make the man - or woman! Although hairstyle, grooming and body odour will be important indicators to an interviewee's mind set, the 'uniform' he or she wears will tell you most about the image they are trying to project.

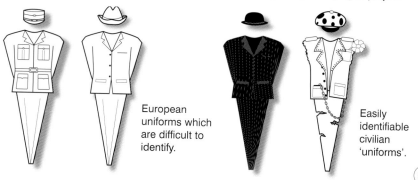

European uniforms which are difficult to identify.

Easily identifiable civilian 'uniforms'.

EXPRESSIONS OF EMOTION

Studies by Davitz give good news to interviewers! The best way to judge the feelings and emotions of interviewees is to watch their faces.

Facial expressions convey emotions with much more accuracy than voice tone or, even, body posture.

So, when in doubt about how interviewees feel during an interview, watch their faces and trust your own judgement!

FURTHER READING

'**Precision**', McMaster & Grinder, Precision Models

'**Making People Talk**', John Townsend, Journal of European Industrial Training, Volume 10, Number 8

'**Paralinguistics**', John Townsend, Journal of European Industrial Training, Volume 9, Number 3

'**Messages**', McKay, Davis & Fanning, New Harbinger

'**Bodily Communication**', Michael Argyle, Routledge

'**Body Language**', 3rd ed'n, Alan Pease, Sheldon Press

NOTES

PART 2: INTERVIEW TYPES & TIPS
THE SELECTION INTERVIEW

THE SELECTION INTERVIEW

PREPARATION

Why is good selection interviewing important?

Success	**Your** success depends on the quality of the people you hire.
Cost	Selection mistakes can cost thousands - in advertising/agency fees and replacement costs such as severance pay, lost sales, training costs, etc.
Growth	Your organisation's growth depends on your ability to attract and keep good people.
Reputation	The selection interview is a dialogue with the labour market. The way you conduct interviews will be fed back to the market and create (or destroy) a reputation.
Development	If you select mediocre people you can't develop them into future leaders.

THE SELECTION INTERVIEW

PREPARATION
CANDIDATE DATA SHEET

Whether you are interviewing internal or external candidates for a vacant position, you will need a written data sheet on each candidate before you begin the interviewing process.

There are three kinds of candidate data sheet:

1. Standardised application form   -   External candidate
2. Typed CV/résumé   -   External candidate
3. Job history/personal file   -   Internal candidate

Whichever you choose, ensure that you have consistent data on each candidate.

THE SELECTION INTERVIEW

PREPARATION
JOB DESCRIPTIONS 1

An up-to-date job description is essential for a good selection interview. Otherwise, how can you give a true picture of the job? If you don't have one, there's a risk that some parts of the job which you discuss in the interview later turn out not to be in the job; or tasks which are not mentioned come to light only when the candidate starts.

Without one, the candidate will be **disappointed, frustrated, incompetent** or **scared** when he or she begins.

THE SELECTION INTERVIEW

PREPARATION
JOB DESCRIPTIONS 2

A good job description covers at least four elements of the job:

1. Accountabilities/responsibilities/duties
A checklist of the activities for which the position holder is responsible.

2. Dimensions
The **level** or **size** of the responsibility (ie: sales, budget, people responsibility, functional reports, capital equipment)

3. Framework
Where does the job fit in the organisation (organigram)?

4. Relationships
With whom does the position holder interact, both inside and outside?

THE SELECTION INTERVIEW

PREPARATION
JOB SPECIFICATION 1

A job specification sets out in **quantifiable** terms the **person requirements** for the job.

Once you know what the job is (job description) then you have to decide what kind of person you need to do it (job specification).

If you have not specified the kind of person you need, how can you judge whether any candidate fits the bill?

To paraphrase the Cheshire Cat in 'Alice in Wonderland', 'If you don't know where you're going, any road will take you there!'.

PREPARATION

JOB SPECIFICATION 2

There are many ways of structuring a good job specification.

Here is one which many selection interviewers have found useful.

JOB SPECIFICATION

Physical
- Health
- Appearance

Achievements
- Education
- Experience
- Training

Aptitudes
- Equipment
- Words
- Figures

Disposition
- Acceptability
- Persuasiveness
- Dependability
- Initiative

Environment
- Domestic
- Background

Interests/hobbies

Salary requirements

THE SELECTION INTERVIEW

PREPARATION

QUANTIFYING THE JOB SPECIFICATION

Professional selection interviewers know that you can only make good selection decisions when candidates can be measured objectively against quantifiable specifications.

Example for a sales rep

Physical	● Health	- Doctor's certificate shows no major problems
	● Appearance	- Dress/grooming at least equal to present sales staff
Achievements	● Education	- Minimum high school; maximum BA/BSc
	● Experience	- At least five years' sales experience
	● Training	- At least two sales training courses

PREPARATION

QUANTIFYING THE JOB SPECIFICATION (Cont'd)

Aptitudes	• Equipment	- Has previously worked with XYZ software
	• Words	- Can produce a report written by self
	• Figures	- Can calculate a 12.5% discount on the spot
Disposition	• Acceptability	- Could be sent to customer X tomorrow
	• Persuasiveness	- Can sell a gadget on the spot
	• Dependability	- Absentee record within company average
	• Initiative	- Two examples of self-starting
Environment	• Domestic	- No evidence of major crisis at present
	• Background	- No obvious 'class hang-ups'
Interests/hobbies		- Evidence of healthy outside interests
Salary requirements		- Present salary below X

THE SELECTION INTERVIEW

PREPARATION

SHORT-LISTING

Short-listing consists of choosing 3-5 candidates to interview from the total applications available.

In many organisations this is the job of the personnel department.

Short-listing involves comparing each application to the job specification and selecting those 'paper' candidates who seem to fit best.

NB If the application contains insufficient data then ask for more or give the benefit of the doubt and short-list for an interview.

PREPARATION

PLANNING INTERVIEW COVERAGE 1

Some of the
information
required
in order to rate
candidates against
the job specification
cannot be obtained
during an interview
but only from
reference checks,
medical certificates,
etc.

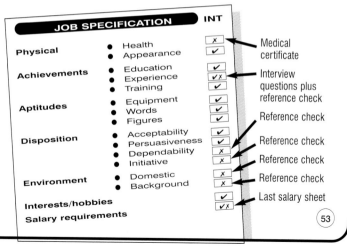

JOB SPECIFICATION		INT	
Physical	• Health	x	Medical certificate
	• Appearance	✔	
Achievements	• Education	✔	
	• Experience	✔x	Interview questions plus reference check
	• Training	✔	
Aptitudes	• Equipment	✔	
	• Words	✔	
	• Figures	✔	
Disposition	• Acceptability	✔	Reference check
	• Persuasiveness	x	Reference check
	• Dependability	x	Reference check
	• Initiative	x	Reference check
Environment	• Domestic	x	Reference check
	• Background	x	
Interests/hobbies		✔	Last salary sheet
Salary requirements		✔x	

THE SELECTION INTERVIEW

PREPARATION
PLANNING INTERVIEW COVERAGE 2

Everybody (including you) tries to look as good as possible on their CV/résumé.

When preparing for your interview note down (on the candidate's papers) any questions*
you have on:

- Seemingly incomplete or blown-up educational achievements
- Seemingly exaggerated job titles/responsibilities
- Missing months/years
- Image-strengthening hobbies
- Salary requirements versus present earnings

* and, perhaps, **how** you are going to ask them

THE SELECTION INTERVIEW

PREPARATION

PREPARING THE INTERVIEW ROOM

Checklist*

- Mirror on the wall of waiting area
- Clock on wall of interviewing room (behind candidate)
- No telephone interruptions/knocks on door
- No bright sunlight in candidate's eyes
- Application + job description + job specification + preparatory notes + interview notepad at ready
- Company/organisational literature to hand

* If it's good enough for Lufthansa, it's good enough for you!

THE SELECTION INTERVIEW

INTERVIEW STRUCTURE
PUTTING THE CANDIDATE AT EASE

Greeting

Be warm and friendly. Get up, come over to shake hands. Small talk on weather/trip/building/parking, etc.

Remember, the candidate is always nervous. The most successful interviews are those where the interviewer begins by showing the candidate that, if there is to be a psychologically superior person in the interview, **it will be the candidate**.

INTERVIEW STRUCTURE

PUTTING THE CANDIDATE AT EASE (Cont'd)

First moves

- If possible, sit with candidate and mirror body posture (see page 25)
- Ask what time candidate must get away
- Tell candidate that the purpose of the interview is to help him or her decide whether this is the right job
- Leave 'selling' the job until the end

Example

'Our objective here is to get to know each other as well as possible in the short time available, so I'd like to start by asking you to tell me as much as possible about yourself and then I'll do my best to talk about me, the job and the organisation. After all, someone's got to start: OK? Perhaps you could first tell me something about ...'

THE SELECTION INTERVIEW

INTERVIEW STRUCTURE

QUESTIONS & ANSWERS

After your opening remarks the interview should follow the 7-point structure, with questions being asked and answers being provided on **each item** (education, experience, etc) of the job specification **which you have planned to cover**.

Vary your questioning technique according to the subject under discussion and the reactions of the candidate (see 'questioning techniques', pages 5-14).

INTERVIEW STRUCTURE

FLOOR TIME

The 30/70 rule
A basic rule for 'floor time' during
a selection interview is that
the candidate speaks for
70% of the time and you
speak for only 30% of
the time. After all,
who's the one being
interviewed?!

THE SELECTION INTERVIEW

EVALUATING THE CANDIDATES

USING A DECISION MATRIX

The most objective way to evaluate candidates is to rate each of them against each item on the job specification.

The candidate with the highest score may not be the one you eventually hire - but at least you know the reasons for your selection.

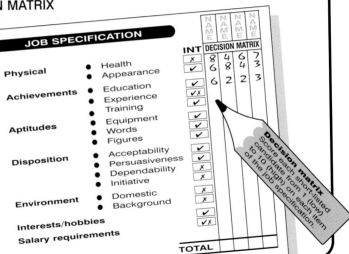

JOB SPECIFICATION		INT	DECISION MATRIX
			NAME NAME NAME NAME
Physical	Health	X	8 4 6 7
	Appearance	✔	6 8 4 3
Achievements	Education	✔	6 2 2 3
	Experience	✔X	
	Training	✔	
Aptitudes	Equipment	✔	
	Words	✔	
	Figures	✔	
Disposition	Acceptability	✔	
	Persuasiveness	✔	
	Dependability	X	
	Initiative	X	
Environment	Domestic	X	
	Background	X	
Interests/hobbies		✔	
Salary requirements		✔X	
		TOTAL	

Decision matrix
Score each short-listed candidate from 1 (low) to 10 (high) on each item of the job specification.

THE SELECTION INTERVIEW

FOLLOW-UP: REFERENCE CHECKS

Never hire a candidate without checking references.
Some golden rules for reference checking:

- Don't rely on testimonials or references given by a candidate - ask a given referee for other referees and contact them.

- Always try and contact referees by **phone**, not in writing.

- Phone technique:
  - Ask a general question but don't bother to listen to the answer.
  - Pinpoint a possibly negative item from your interview with the candidate and ask referee to comment. Repeat as necessary and listen to **how** the answer is given.
  - Finish by asking 'Would you re-hire this person if he/she came back to you for a job?' Be wary of any hesitation. Referees can **always** find a job for top ex-performers.

THE SELECTION INTERVIEW

FOLLOW-UP: OUTCOME LETTERS

Always follow up on each interview by informing the candidate of the outcome of the interview.

- Thanks but no thanks (dead file)
- Not now but maybe later (active file)
- Still too early for decision (pending)
- Next step (ie: second interview)
- Contract in mail soon

NB The reputation of your organisation is closely bound to the way you treat ex-candidates.

PART 2: INTERVIEW TYPES & TIPS
THE APPRAISAL INTERVIEW

THE APPRAISAL INTERVIEW

PROBLEMS IN APPRAISING PERFORMANCE

Appraisers are faced with several built-in barriers. They:

- Lack sufficient relevant information
- Make up their minds too quickly
- Decide more on the basis of opinion than fact
- Project their own values and standards on subordinates
- Don't want to relinquish power or authority

But, they also dislike playing God!

THE APPRAISAL INTERVIEW

PRINCIPLES OF PERFORMANCE APPRAISAL

One way to overcome appraisal barriers is to use the:

S O S +  **APPROACH**

Standards
Objectives
Self-appraisal

1 Achievements
2 Limitations
3 Improvement
4 Potential
5 Development

THE APPRAISAL INTERVIEW

S O S + 5 APPROACH

S O S represents the three main **principles** that should govern a good appraisal interview:

Standards   Performance should be discussed in the light of the standard of
work expected for each item of the job accountabilities.

Objectives   Any specific objectives agreed upon for the period under
discussion should be reviewed in detail.

Self-appraisal Whenever possible the interviewee should give his or her own
appraisal of performance.

THE APPRAISAL INTERVIEW

S O S + 5 APPROACH

The appraisal interview will be much easier if the appraisee's objectives - set at the beginning of the review period - meet three criteria and have three components.

HOW TO SET A GOOD OBJECTIVE		
MUST MEET 3 CRITERIA	**Necessary**	Represents a critical difference in expected performance
	Realistic	Is believed attainable by boss and doer
	Agreed	Has been agreed by boss and doer
MUST HAVE 3 COMPONENTS	**Result**	To be achieved
	Deadline	By when, specifically?
	Limits	Without ...? Provided that ...?
ACTION PLAN/ STEPS		Sub-objectives or 'labour pains'

THE APPRAISAL INTERVIEW

S O S + 5 APPROACH

The five points represent the ideal **structure** of a good appraisal interview:

1 Achievements   First discuss the appraisee's major accomplishments. Show appreciation. Give praise. Encourage.

2 Limitations   Next establish what prevented the appraisee achieving missed standards and objectives.

3 Improvement   Help the appraisee to find ways of doing **even** better.

4 Potential   Agree on the **kind** of future the appraisee can expect within the organisation based on past performance. (**No promises!**)

5 Development   Help the appraisee find ways of achieving this growth.

INTERVIEW STYLE

As with any modern management technique, experience has shown that there is no **one** best way to conduct an appraisal interview. You will adapt your style according to your own situation and the appraisee's personality and performance level:

YOU

- Experience
- Personality
- Service
- Style

APPRAISEE + APPRAISEE'S PERFORMANCE

- Experience
- Personality
- Service
- Circumstances
- Level of performance

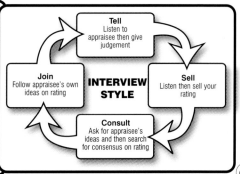

INTERVIEW STYLE

Tell — Listen to appraisee then give judgement

Sell — Listen then sell your rating

Consult — Ask for appraisee's ideas and then search for consensus on rating

Join — Follow appraisee's own ideas on rating

THE APPRAISAL INTERVIEW

INTERVIEW TIPS 1

THE 'TWO OUTCOME MIND SET'

By the end of any performance appraisal interview you should have made the appraisee feel either:

- Motivated to do better (or even better!)

  or, in the case of unacceptable performance:

- Motivated to leave the organisation

YES!

THE APPRAISAL INTERVIEW

INTERVIEW TIPS 2
THE HAMBURGER TECHNIQUE

Most people will accept critique much more readily if they already know where they've done well - especially if that critique is followed by some more good news, So, when rating performance:

GOOD NEWS

BAD NEWS

GOOD NEWS

Start by highlighting achievements. Show appreciation. Be specific.

Follow with a discussion regarding an unsatisfactory area of performance. Be specific.

Quickly identify another area of performance with which you are pleased. Show appreciation. Be specific.

THE APPRAISAL INTERVIEW

INTERVIEW TIPS 3

Do:

- Choose a quiet place and appropriate time
- Allow adequate time (in most cases you will need up to 90 minutes)
- Use all the questioning techniques (see pages 5-14)
- 'Close' on each issue before moving to the next
- Agree on remedial action for each problem area
- Summarise the interview and agree on action plan

INTERVIEW TIPS 4

Don't:

- Rate isolated incidents
- Allow the 'halo' effect (where good performance in one area masks inadequate performance in others) to bias your rating
- Allow the 'Lucifer' effect (where bad performance in an area masks good performance in others) to bias your rating
- Bargain on ratings
- Only give bad news

Don't talk ... listen!
(Ideal: appraisee 60%, appraiser 40%)

NOTES

PART 2: INTERVIEW TYPES & TIPS
THE DISCIPLINE INTERVIEW

DEFINITION/PRINCIPLE

All too often managers see a discipline interview as an obligation to punish or 'read the riot act' to an employee who has broken the rules.

The first meaning of discipline in the dictionary is 'training'; the last is to 'punish'.

So, the principle of a discipline interview is that the interviewer should concentrate on training for correction.

Punishment may be the end result but only when the training for correction has failed.

> discipline.
> **discipline** (**dis**-i-plin) *n.* **1**. training that produces obedience, self-control, or a particular skill. **2**. controlled behaviour produced by such training. **3**. punishment given to correct a person or enforce obedience. **4**. a branch of instruction or learning. ——**discipline** *v.* **1**. to train to be obedient and orderly. **2**. to punish.
> **disclaim** *v.* to disown; *they disclaim re-*

THE DISCIPLINE INTERVIEW

THE SNAP METHOD

The **SNAP** method for dealing with discipline and other delicate uncomfortable behavioural situations has been developed from over 20 years of personnel management experience. The secret of its success is that it allows the interviewer to combine neutrality and feeling.

S pecify the behaviour or situation you wish to change

N ame yourself, the interviewee and all others involved

A sk for a feasible and specific change; affirm the rules

P ropose a 'prize' for change and/or a 'penalty' for no change

THE SNAP METHOD

S pecify   Describe the behaviour or situation you wish to change in a **neutral** manner.

- Concentrate on facts (be prepared) and specify the gap between the present behaviour and desired behaviour
- Avoid any value judgement at this stage
- Where possible use the 'passive' tense ('It is on record that ...' 'These figures show ...')
- Don't suggest or insinuate - state facts
- Discuss the facts until the interviewee agrees (or at least acquiesces)
- If you can't get agreement on facts, postpone the interview until you have got the facts right

THE DISCIPLINE INTERVIEW

THE SNAP METHOD

Name   Name yourself, the interviewee and all others involved.

- Say how you **feel** about the behaviour/situation
- Share your views on how others feel
- Discuss the interviewee's feelings/emotions
- Probe for reasons for the undesired behaviour/situation
- Show empathy and concern where necessary
- Keep it personal (**I**, **you**, **we**); not 'the company' or 'management'
- Do not move on to 'A' until there is a consensus on feelings

  Use the 'broken record' technique:
  - 'Yes, that's why I feel so angry with you ...'
  - 'OK, so you're saying you **do** feel upset ...'

THE DISCIPLINE INTERVIEW

THE SNAP METHOD

Ask Ask for a feasible and specific change in behaviour. Affirm the rules.

- Be specific
- Set a deadline
- Be creative, use empathy, give reasons
- Use a friendly but firm tone of voice

Before the interviewee can react ...

THE DISCIPLINE INTERVIEW

THE SNAP METHOD

Propose   A prize or pay off if the interviewee changes behaviour and/or a penalty if he or she doesn't.

Prize or pay off:
- Show what will happen if change takes place
- Offer a reward, however small
- Say what **you** will do if change takes place
- Show benefits to interviewee of changing
- Underline benefits of change to relationships
- Show benefits to the organisation

Penalty or punishment:
- Clarify the consequences of unchanged behaviour (to you, others, interviewee, the organisation)
- Be bold, clear and precise

THE DISCIPLINE INTERVIEW

SNAP DELIVERY TECHNIQUE

S ▶ N Do not move to naming people and feelings until you have some kind of agreement on the facts.

N ▶ A Do not ask for anything until you have consensus on feelings and on the reasons behind the situation.

A ▶ P **Do not pause between asking and proposing.**

Why? Because otherwise you may get an argument on the change you want. This is not negotiable. If you go straight to 'proposing' without pausing, any argument will be on the pay off or punishment. This may be negotiable **if** change occurs.

THE DISCIPLINE INTERVIEW

SNAP DELIVERY TECHNIQUE

EXAMPLE: LATECOMING

Specify 'Mary, I have your time sheets here and they show that you've been over 30 minutes late for the office six times during the last two weeks. We are staffed at the minimum and have a lot of backlog in order processing. You agreed to abide by company rules when you signed your contract.'
(Discussion on reasons)

Name 'I understand you have problems getting the kids to school. Nevertheless, I get angry when I see you arriving late because it's unfair to the other employees who are making the effort.'

Ask 'So, starting Monday, I want you to have found a solution for the kids/school problem and arrive on time for 10 consecutive days. We'll review timekeeping two weeks on Monday.'

Propose *Pay off:* 'If you show me you can do it I'll stop feeling angry and the others will stop feeling resentment at your late-coming.'

Penalty: 'If not, I'll have to give you a written warning and you may lose your job.'

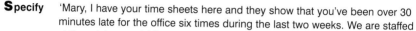

(83)

ENDING THE INTERVIEW

As soon as you have obtained a 'contract' concerning the pay off and/or penalty for change it is time to end the interview.

1. Confirm agreement and review date.

2. Smile, shake hands and shut up!

3. Make a written résumé of interview:
   - one copy for file
   - one copy for interviewee.

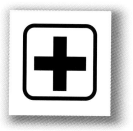

PART 2: INTERVIEW TYPES & TIPS
THE COUNSELLING INTERVIEW

THE COUNSELLING INTERVIEW

THE NATURE OF HELPING

Managers are called upon to counsel employees as often as employees need **help**.

A need for help can be manifested in many ways - from a serious need for psychotherapeutic treatment through a temporary need to let off emotional steam to a simple need for a sympathetic ear in discussing career prospects, etc.

The **WRAF** approach suggested in this chapter may be applied to all these situations with the proviso that a psychologically disturbed interviewee will probably also need professional treatment.

THE COUNSELLING INTERVIEW

THE WRAF APPROACH

British readers will know that **WRAF** is the acronym for the **W**omen's **R**oyal **A**ir **F**orce. I don't know if this organisation uses the suggested approach to counselling - but it's a useful mnemonic device!

W
- Welcoming

R
- Reflective listening
- Reflecting body postures
- Reframing

A
- Action planning

F
- Following-up

THE COUNSELLING INTERVIEW

THE WRAF APPROACH

STEP 1

Welcoming

Whenever an employee comes to you with a counselling problem (**or** whenever **you** decide it is necessary to conduct a counselling interview) the 'welcome' is all-important:

- Do everything in your power to create a climate of trust and lack of threat (time, place, preamble, body language).

- Express **positive regard** for interviewee. Show readiness to **listen** and to **help**.

- Illustrate **compassion/empathy** with examples and, if necessary, defuse any guilt with revelation of your own inadequacies.

THE COUNSELLING INTERVIEW

THE WRAF APPROACH

STEP 2

Reflective listening (see also page 10)

The most effective way to listen to an interviewee who needs any kind of help is to use the **R**ogerian method of reflective or active listening (Carl Rogers).

After each of the interviewee's statements, reflect back what you think you have heard:

- 'You feel frustrated when your boss doesn't seem to listen to you?'
- 'If I understand correctly, you don't feel we've done enough to train you?'
- 'In other words, he implied that you were lazy and unco-operative?'

Golden Rule   Don't suggest solutions or give advice at this stage. Reflect what you hear.

Why?   The interviewee will soon start suggesting own solutions!

THE COUNSELLING INTERVIEW

THE WRAF APPROACH

STEP 2 (Cont'd)

Reflecting body postures (see also page 25)

You can instil a climate of openness by 'mirroring' an interviewee's body postures. Intuitively he or she feels that you are on the same wavelength.

- Adopt same sitting position (legs, arms, leaning, etc)
- Adapt body posture as interviewee changes
- Mirror hand and arm gestures with 'micro-mimicry' (ie: if interviewee flails arms, you imitate the movements with your hands/fingers)

THE COUNSELLING INTERVIEW

THE WRAF APPROACH

STEP 2 (Cont'd)

Reframing

Reframing consists of putting the information provided by the interviewee into another context or framework.

Example

Employee	'But, I guess it's right when my boss says that I'm a slow worker. I put in a hell of a lot of effort but I never seem to be able to meet deadlines.'
Interviewer	'You prefer to produce high quality work a bit late than mediocre work which is bang on time?'
Employee	'Well, yes, that's true, I suppose.'

THE COUNSELLING INTERVIEW

THE WRAF APPROACH

STEP 3

Action planning

When counselling friends or acquaintances in a domestic situation, it is sometimes sufficient just to lend a sympathetic ear and maybe make a few helpful, if vague, suggestions.

However, in an on-the-job counselling interview it is essential to agree on an action plan with the interviewee.

Ideally, the interviewee should be helped into proposing his or her own actions (eg: Interviewer: 'It sounds like you're saying that you'd like to ...'). Failing this, the interviewer may propose actions provided they echo what he or she feels are the interviewee's own thoughts, and as long as they are feasible.

| **Examples of specific action to be taken** | To talk to boss about criticism. To visit doctor. To make an appointment with therapist. To enrol in evening course. To look at three houses which are nearer the office. |

THE COUNSELLING INTERVIEW

THE WRAF APPROACH

STEP 4

Follow-up

Before terminating a counselling interview you should agree with the interviewee not only on a date on which you will meet again to review that action plan, but also on the kind of follow-up actions that might ensue.

Psychologically, this 2-step approach ensures that:

a) The interviewee takes his or her action commitments seriously (because something else depends on the action result).

b) The consequences of not fulfilling the action plan are clear right from the start.

Example of action plan and follow-up	'So, we've agreed that you will enrol in a PC course by July 31st and meet to review your commitment on August 5th. Otherwise, we'll have to conclude that your career is limited to filing and clerical work.'

NOTES

PART 2: INTERVIEW TYPES & TIPS
THE FACT-FINDING INTERVIEW

THE FACT-FINDING INTERVIEW

DEFINITIONS/OBJECTIVES

When an interviewer decides to conduct a fact-finding session with an information-giver, he or she usually has one of three objectives:

1. Facilitation/Arbitration To encourage one or more interviewees to provide specific information which **they** can then use in order to solve problems.

2. Interrogation To 'get to the bottom' of things by cross-examining an interviewee to obtain information on which to base future decisions.

3. Surveying To obtain consistent information from several interviewees using a pre-prepared questionnaire.

THE FACT-FINDING INTERVIEW

QUESTIONING TECHNIQUES

With the exception of the surveying interview (for which questions are prepared in advance on a questionnaire) the key questions to ask are:

Blockbusting questions   Noun, verb, universal, comparator
(see page 8)

Challenge questions   Evidence, missing link, devil's advocate
(see page 12)

Framing questions   Outcome frame, backtrack frame, relevance frame
(see page 13)

Reflective questions   Reflecting back what you think you heard
(see page 10)

Silence   (see page 14)

THE FACT-FINDING INTERVIEW

ADDITIONAL SKILLS

Although the fact-finding interview is, by definition, focusing on facts, the skilled interviewer will smooth out the cold, analytical process by using two additional techniques:

1. Factual linking   Building links or bridges between the information being provided and the areas of concern of the interviewer.

Evidence challenge example
'You mentioned just now that one of your objectives is to create a team spirit within the department. I'd be interested in hearing about the kind of measurement you'll use to judge how successful you've been.'

2. Empathetic prefacing   Showing interest and concern about the information being provided.

Verb blockbusting example
'It sounds like you're going through a tough time in your division. Tell me, how specifically are you dealing with the communication problem?'

THE FACT-FINDING INTERVIEW

FACILITATION EXAMPLE

		Questioning Technique
Interviewee	*'Of course, my biggest problem is improving the morale in the department. None of the workers seems to care about quality.'*	
Interviewer	'None of them?'	**Universal blockbuster**
Interviewee	*'Well, some of them take their jobs seriously - but Joe Blake's group don't seem to care. They're just not motivated.'*	
Interviewer	'I'd be interested in **how** they don't seem motivated?'	**Verb blockbuster**
Interviewee	*'They're always complaining about things - not pulling their weight. As I say, we've got to improve the morale.'*	
Interviewer	'Yeah. It's important all right but ...er, what will you accept as evidence that morale **has** improved?'	**Evidence challenge**

continued ...

FACILITATION EXAMPLE (Cont'd)

		Questioning Technique
Interviewee	'Well, the reject figure for a start. Joe Blake's group hit 6% rejects last month for the first time ever, and absenteeism, too - they never seem to be there on Mondays and Fridays.'	
Interviewer	'What is the absenteeism rate, exactly?'	**Noun blockbuster**
Interviewee	'I haven't got the exact figure but it's pretty high.'	
Interviewer	'Yes, I agree that's disturbing. How is absenteeism compared with other sections?'	**Comparator**
Interviewee	'Oh, must be 3-4% more.'	
Interviewer	'OK. How can we frame this problem as an objective... I mean, what outcome would you like to see?'	**Outcome frame**
Interviewee	'Well, we'll have to reduce both rejects and absenteeism and I guess **you** should talk to Joe Blake about his management style. He's very autocratic with his people.'	

THE FACT-FINDING INTERVIEW

FACILITATION EXAMPLE (Cont'd)

		Questioning Technique
Interviewer	'Sorry, help me to see how my intervention would help?'	**Relevance frame**
Interviewee	*'Well, you're the big boss! At least he'll listen to you!'*	
Interviewer	'Mmm. What would you argue against my involvement?'	**Devil's advocate challenge**
Interviewee	*'Yes, well, I guess I am his supervisor. No, I think I should talk to him first.'*	
Interviewer	'OK. Good idea. Now, what else seems to be a factor in the high rejects and absenteeism?'	**Missing link challenge**
Interviewee	*'Uh ... could be the new micro-processor control unit. They don't like all this hi-tech stuff.'*	
Interviewer	'OK. Let's recap on the facts of the situation. Rejects are 6%. Absenteeism is 3-4% over the norm. If I understand you correctly, Joe Blake's management style may be at the root of it or it might be the lack of acceptance of the micro-processor?'	**Reflective question**

FURTHER READING

'**Influencing with Integrity**', Genie Laborde, Syntony

'**The Structure of Magic**' **(I & II),** Bandler & Grinder, Science and Behaviour Books

'**The Art of Helping**', R. Carkhuff, H.R.D.

'**On Becoming a Person**', Carl Rogers, Constable

'**Face to Face**', 2nd ed'n, Peter Honey, Gower

'**Analyzing Performance Problems**', 2nd ed'n, R. Mager & P. Pike, Kogan Page

PART 3: SKILLS SUMMARIES
QUESTIONING TECHNIQUES
INTERACTIVE LISTENING
<u>BODY LANGUAGE</u>

QUESTIONING TECHNIQUES (CLOSED)

Type of Questions	EXAMPLES	WHEN TO ASK
MULTIPLE	A string of several questions at once	• NEVER
LEADING	Questions which indicate the desired response • 'Ah, I see you worked for XYZ International?' • 'Of course, no health problems, eh?'	• NEVER
PROBING	• 'How old were you then?' • 'What are the sales of ABC Inc?' • 'How many employees were there at that time?'	• When interviewee is rambling/talking too much • When you wish to probe for facts or details of accomplishments
BLOCKBUSTING Noun Action Universal Comparator	• 'Which/what (noun) specifically?' • 'How (verb) exactly?' • 'All?' 'Never?' 'Did everyone think that?' • 'Compared to what?'	• When you want 'high quality' information on specific things or actions • After vague, universal statements like 'all', 'none', 'everybody', 'always', 'never' • After statements using vague comparisons like 'better', 'increase', 'improve', 'less', 'more efficient', etc

QUESTIONING TECHNIQUES (**OPEN**)

Type of Questions	EXAMPLES	WHEN TO ASK
'ABOUT' QUESTIONS	• 'Tell me more about ...' • 'What do you think about ...?' • 'How do you feel about ...?'	• At the beginning of an interview to get interviewee talking • When you wish to hear the interviewee's opinions, attitudes or beliefs
REFLECTIVE	Reflecting back a statement of what you think you heard • 'You seem to feel upset with ...?' • 'If I understand correctly, you ...?' • 'In other words, you don't ...?' • 'You thought perhaps he was over-reacting?'	• When the interviewee is emotionally involved in what is being discussed • When discussing complex matters • When interviewee is incoherent
HYPOTHETICAL	• 'What would you do if ...?' • 'Could we role-play this situation? I'll be the customer/student.' • 'What could have happened if ...?'	• When you wish to test creativity and/or the ability to think quickly and logically • To test selling or public speaking skills

QUESTIONING TECHNIQUES (**OPEN**)

Type of Questions	EXAMPLES	WHEN TO ASK
CHALLENGE		
Evidence	• 'What will you accept as evidence that you have succeeded?'	• To test interviewee's approach to objectives/targets
Missing Link	• 'What do you think was missing from the system?'	• To probe interviewee's analytical abilities
Devil's Advocate	• 'What counter-arguments can you think of?'	• A way of challenging the interviewee's objectivity
FRAMING		
Outcome Frame	• 'What is the real objective/outcome you are aiming at?'	• To test planning ability and probe reasons for actions
Backtrack Frame	• 'Let's backtrack a moment. How did you see things at the time?'	• To help put information in 'context'
Relevance Frame	• 'Help me to see how this fits in with ...?'	• When you can't see why a point was brought up but want to get the interview back on track by giving benefit of doubt
SILENCE		• To draw out reticent, timid interviewees • To obtain information you think is being withheld

INTERACTIVE LISTENING

PREPARING TO LISTEN

- Ask yourself: 'What new things can I learn from this person?' Be selfish!

  "There is no such thing as an uninteresting subject.
  There are only uninterested people." *G.K. Chesterton*

- Mentally review the 'listening barriers' and pinpoint your own bad habits.

- Actively move away from distractions. 'Perhaps we could go and sit in the corner/use a free office/go into the kitchen.'

- Lean forward, establish sensitive eye contact and show you're ready to listen.

THE 30 SECOND RULE

**When you are speaking,
try and pause about every 30 seconds
to allow your partner to interrupt,
comment or give you a sign to continue.**

Remember:

	Learned	Used	Taught
Listening	First	Most (45%)	Least
Speaking	Second	Next most (30%)	Next least
Reading	Third	Next least (16%)	Next most
Writing	Last	Least (9%)	Most

LISTENING BARRIERS

1. **Scoring 'points'** (Relating everything you hear to your own experience)
   - Saying, 'Oh, that's nothing, you should have seen what happened to me last week!'
   - Thinking, 'My kids are so much more intelligent/better behaved!'

2. **Mind reading** (Predicting what the speaker is really thinking)
   - Thinking, 'I bet he doesn't give a damn for what I think.'

3. **Rehearsing** (Practising your next lines in your head)
   - Waiting to tell your story - and practising the punch line

4. **Cherry picking** (Listening for a key piece of information - then switching off)
   - Checking if someone is in a good mood, then allowing thoughts to wander
   - Hearing a project has been finished then tuning out as she or he tells how

5. **Daydreaming**
   - You can think 4-6 times faster than people can talk. The temptation is to use the 'spare' time to daydream.

6. **Labelling** (Putting a speaker into a category before hearing all the evidence)
   - Quickly dubbing a speaker as a fascist, immoral, effeminate, etc
   - Not listening to someone whom you've decided is stupid, etc

7. **Counselling** (Being unable to resist interrupting and giving advice)
   - Saying, 'Why don't you try ...' or 'In my experience, the best ...'

8. **Duelling**
   (Countering the speaker's verbal advances with parries and thrusts of your own)
   - Saying, 'Well, at least our department wasn't over budget!'
   - Saying, 'Don't blame me; it was your idea in the first place.'

9. **Side-stepping sentiment**
   (Countering expressions of emotion with jokes or hollow clichés)
   - Saying, 'Well, it's not the end of the world, is it?'
   - Saying, 'Stiff upper lip. Tomorrow's another day!'

INTERACTIVE LISTENING

Maintain Sensitive Eye Contact
EUROPEAN AVERAGE
- Individual gaze while listening = 75% of time
- Mutual eye contact = 30% of time
- Length of mutual glance = 1.5 seconds

Try and 'Mirror' the Speaker's Body Posture and Talking Speed
(unless you feel unnatural)

Encourage the Speaker to Continue When You Want More Information
- 'That's interesting, go on ...'
- 'Tell me some more about ...'

Paraphrase Regularly
(Use Reflective Questioning technique)
- 'What I hear you saying is ...'
- 'In other words, you ...'
- 'So, if I understand you correctly ...'

Clarify Information
(Use other questioning techniques)
- Probing and blockbusting • Challenging and framing • Hypothetical questions

If it's important – make a note of it

Give regular feedback on how you feel
- Process: 'I'm glad we can talk about this openly today'
- Content: 'I share some of your views on XYZ, but I also think that ...'

HOW TO READ BODY LANGUAGE

HANDS

Steepling
Self-confidence (intellectual arrogance?)

Hand clasp
Anxious, controlled

Nose touch
Doubt

'L' chin rest
Critical evaluation

Mouth block
Resisting speech

SITTING

Arms up
Reserved, defensive

Arm/leg cross
Closed, unconvinced

Lean forward
Ready!

Lean back
Confident superiority

Lint-picking
Disapproval

STANDING

Thumbs out
In charge! Dominant

Fig leaf
Self-control, tense

Arms out/palms up
Open, sincere, conciliatory

Table lean
Authoritative, involved

Lean on
Unthreatened, casual belongingness

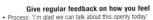

About the Author

John Townsend, BA, MA, MCIPD

John is Managing Director of the Master Trainer Institute. He founded the Institute after 30 years of experience in international consulting and human resource management positions in the UK, France, the United States and Switzerland.

From 1978-1984 he was European Director of Executive Development with GTE in Geneva with training responsibility for over 800 managers in some 15 countries. Mr Townsend has published a number of management and professional guides and regularly contributes articles to leading management and training journals.

In addition to training trainers, he is also a regular speaker at conferences and leadership seminars throughout Europe.

John Townsend can be contacted at:

The Master Trainer Institute, L'Avant Centre, 13 chemin du Levant, Ferney-Voltaire, France
Tel: (33) 450 42 84 16   Fax: (33) 450 40 57 37   Website: www.mt-institute.com

Published by: Management Pocketbooks Ltd., Laurel House, Station Approach, Alresford, Hants SO24 9JH, U.K. Tel: +44 (0)1962 735573   Fax: +44 (0)1962 733637

Editions: 1st: 1987, Reprinted 1993, 1995, 1996, 1997 2nd: 1999, 2000, 2002, 2004, 2005.
All rights reserved. © John Townsend 1987 and 1999   ISBN 1 870471 75 X   Printed in the UK

British Library Cataloguing-in-Publication Data – A catalogue record for this book is available from the British Library

ORDER FORM

Your details

Name _____

Position _____

Company _____

Address _____

_____

_____

Telephone _____

Fax _____

E-mail _____

VAT No. (EC companies) _____

Your Order Ref _____

Please send me:

		No. copies
The Interviewer's	Pocketbook	
The _____	Pocketbook	
The _____	Pocketbook	
The _____	Pocketbook	
The _____	Pocketbook	

Order by Post

MANAGEMENT POCKETBOOKS LTD
LAUREL HOUSE, STATION APPROACH, ALRESFORD,
HAMPSHIRE SO24 9JH UK

Order by Phone, Fax or Internet

Telephone: +44 (0)1962 735573
Facsimile: +44 (0)1962 733637
E-mail: sales@pocketbook.co.uk
Web: www.pocketbook.co.uk

Customers in USA should contact:
Stylus Publishing, LLC, 22883 Quicksilver Drive,
Sterling, VA 20166-2012
Telephone: 703 661 1581 or 800 232 0223
Facsimile: 703 661 1501 E-mail: styluspub@aol.com